SELF COACHING FOR PERSONAL DEVELOPMENT

IT'S NOT ABOUT BEING THE BEST, IT'S ABOUT BEING THE BEST THAT YOU CAN BE

CLAIRE MOODY

JCRM Publishing
Claire & Ralph Moody

Published in 2020 by JCRM Publishing, UK

Designed, Produced and Written Claire and Ralph Moody

ISBN: 979- 8573838410

Self-Coaching For Personal Development : It's Not About Being The Best, It's About Being The Best That You Can Be.

If you would like us to create a bespoke journal or development guide for your organisation or work role, contact us on +44 0800 302 9344.

www.jcrm.shop

Retail enquiries to:

orders@jcrm.shop

Self-Coaching For Personal Development
CLAIRE MOODY

Your FREE Book Is Waiting

Many people struggle with low confidence and low self-esteem, which affects their professional and personal lives. Your thoughts and feelings have a significant impact and this is where issues can manifest. If we don't do something about it, a lack of confidence will hold you back. This book will give you an opportunity to think about your confidence in a different way.

Get your FREE copy:
www.jcrm.shop

For my Family

INTRODUCTION

If we want to improve, personal development is essential for all of us. Having tools and advice can help us significantly in our development and this is where coaching comes in. I have designed this book to provide you with the essential skills that all individuals need to help them develop. Moreover, they are the same skill sets I use when coaching clients and you can implement this knowledge into your everyday life to develop yourself accordingly.

If used correctly, this book will aid you in achieving your goals and your dreams. Furthermore, it will help you realise answers to your problems which can be a life changing experience. When using this guide, a good idea is to read each section separately and reflect on yourself afterwards.

As you do this, really notice your thoughts and feelings as you read the page and really notice what this triggers in you. Then write in a journal or diary and finally ask yourself "What would you like to be different?" At the end of this guide I have included some sample journal questions that you may wish to use.

Here's to great success wherever your dreams and ambitions take you.

Claire Moody

IT'S NOT ABOUT BEING THE BEST, IT'S ABOUT BEING THE BEST THAT YOU CAN BE.

1

WHAT IS COACHING?

In my experience coaching is misunderstood, so what is coaching? Coaching is a conversation between a coach and a coachee whereby the coachee achieves a higher level and understanding of awareness and self-awareness, while the coach provides a safe environment and structure for that outcome to occur.

YES, this is a bit of a mouthful, but in essence, it is a process that enables learning and development to occur and thus, performance to improve. To be successful, a coach requires knowledge and understanding of processes well as the variety of styles, skills and techniques that are appropriate to the context in which the coaching takes place. It is about using correct questioning and listening skills. If there is one area that a coach has to master, it is the intent to listen to the coachee, to understand.

To be successful as a coach, you require knowledge and understanding of a variety of skills, style and techniques. This aids coachees to perform to the best of their ability and maximise their performance. I often find myself listening to trainers and mentors who say they have just been delivering a coaching session to a student on a course. When I question them to find out what they have been doing and then check their understanding of what coaching is, I discover that they have no real knowledge of coaching and no real understanding between the roles and techniques required for each. Of course, the way the English language works means coaching is easily misunderstood. What I do know from experience, when coaching is done well it can benefit coachees or members of staff massively in so many areas of their life both professionally and personally. I have experienced individuals managing their team and not using coaching skills. Furthermore, I have witnessed opportunities missed by managers by not listening effectively and not using the guided question technique; essential for effective management. That is why I have put together coaching for managers course to cover techniques and skills which will aid their roles tremendously. I really believe that to be an effective manager you should be able to coach also.

Coaching is proven to increase performance and is now in the majority of professional key sectors. There is a rationale behind this, and it is because it works and you can use the same skills to self-coach.

It is of course understandable why there is so much confusion out there, the English language doesn't help. For example how is it we have a Tennis Coach and a Ski Instructor, you could argue they are doing the same job. In the fields of Learning & Development there specific boundaries though:

MENTORING IS a relationship in which a more experienced or more knowledgeable person, helps to guide a less experienced or less knowledgeable person. It is a learning and development partnership between someone with vast experience and someone who wants to learn.

Workplace examples: - In the workplace mentoring is often conducted when people first start a new job or particular role. For example, you arrive as a project manager and another project manager with lots of experience in the area will look after you. They have occupational competence in the area they are mentoring.

TRAINING IS TEACHING or developing in oneself or others, skills and knowledge that relate to specific useful competencies. Training has specific goals of improving one's capability, capacity, productivity and performance and to maintain, upgrade and update skills throughout working life.

Workplace examples: - In the workplace, training is used widely to pass on skills and knowledge. All managers should also know how to train people; this requires an understanding of the structure of a training session and how to use effective questioning skills.

COUNSELING IS the provision of professional assistance and guidance in resolving personal or psychological problems.

Workplace examples: - Unless you are appropriately qualified you shouldn't be counseling members of staff. Without the correct training, managers who get drawn in can make things worse. There is a thin line sometimes between counseling and management and managers need to be aware of this.

COACHING - THIS IS a conversation between the coach and the coachee, where the coachee achieves a higher level and understanding of awareness and self-awareness. The coach provides a safe environment and structure for that outcome to occur.

Workplace examples: - An essential skill for all managers. Coaching skill sets are required to understand human behavior. It is all about understanding the person, your response to them and how they respond to you. It is about building a relationship that is safe and creating a confidential environment. It is about really listening to understand and not to respond. Managers who coach don't past judgment or tell, they guide.

WHAT WE ARE GOING to do in this guide is understanding coaching skills and using self-coaching for personal development.

2

MAKE MISTAKES, MISTAKES ARE IMPORTANT

Making mistakes is such a massive part of life, and I believe they are not dealt with correctly from an early age. This then can create a fear of making mistakes. Sadly, this then continues through life. Mistakes can form negative thoughts and beliefs that will play out in people's personal and professional lives.

MAKING mistakes can cause self-esteem and confidence problems. The word 'confidence' is such a huge word, and when you ask coachees to talk about the word 'confidence' in their own words, it can create such sadness in their faces and words.

THERE ARE many ways to deal with this as a coach. I sometimes suggest the change of a word and one I have used is to change the word from 'confidence' to 'courage'. This then creates a different approach or idea in a coachee and sometimes can create such a different mindset.

The word 'confidence' can create a lot of negativity. You may be interested to know that we have a **FREE** download called **Developing Courage** which can be downloaded at www.jcrm.shop.

Sadly, making mistakes can hold coachees back in both personal and professional lives. When someone has a superb idea, let's face it most of us in a lifetime will come up with thousands of ideas but will do nothing with them. Sometimes in those ideas will be a million-dollar idea, but most of us will refrain from suggesting it through fear of looking silly. This is where if you create a habit of smiling at responses to your ideas, you will always share your thoughts because it is OK to make mistakes.

I always, with anyone I am 'coaching' or in the past 'training' say "make as many mistakes as you can, enjoy making mistakes". Then, help them learn to deal with the mistakes correctly. Remember, mistakes create creativity, and you can push yourselves in so many ways. Don't hold yourself back. I know I have always done better when I have just scraped through an exam or even failed one by thinking about the subject or myself in a completely different way. I always come away with doing better in the long run because the process in the brain allows this to happen. It is dealing with making mistakes, which is the key.

DO THE THING YOU FEAR MOST FIRST.

3

SHIFT THAT PARADIGM

How often have you reflected on your way of looking at the world? When you change paradigms, you are changing how you think about something.

HAVE you ever reflected on how you view the world and how often someone changes your view of the world? Or maybe not? If not, why? Are you so judgemental in your decisions you choose not to listen subconsciously because you have already made your mind up?

Coaching does help change the way you think about things, a few words by someone else can change the way that you think. Sometimes you wish to change, sometimes not? I often hear, "I wish I could be more like", well you can it is just the way you look at things. It is great to shuffle your paradigm so that you can make some changes.

A paradigm is lots of little habits. Think of the apps on your phone, you have plenty of those apps stored in your subconscious mind. To change or create a new app it requires a repetition of information. Like anything in life, you can change and become an expert by repetition. You must choose to see something differently.

Ask those great questions again, 'what do you want to be different', 'how do you want to be different?' When you watch and think about situations push your boundaries and watch others and how they view the world. Think about the variety of newspapers you can read and how they all report on one situation so differently. It is the same with your situation, how do you want to think about things differently. Force a new app in your subconscious mind, you can do it but sometimes you may need some guidance. Get moving with those paradigms, reflect or be proactive; we don't just do it once, we do it again, again and again until a habit is formed.

YOU CAN'T SOLVE YOUR PROBLEMS BY USING THE SAME THINKING THAT CAUSED THEM IN THE FIRST PLACE - WE HAVE TO THINK DIFFERENTLY.

4

WHEN WE ENCOUNTER
ADVERSITY

I so often hear in my coaching sessions in the language from the coachee sat in front of me that they are struggling with adversity. What do I mean? When we all encounter adversity, we react by thinking about it. These thoughts then rapidly congeal into beliefs. These beliefs then have consequences – they are direct causes of what we feel and do.

Some common comments I hear are :

"I must be perfect, I must get it right, they think I am not good enough, am I good enough to do this,

nobody ever listens to me so why bother, they are annoyed at me and *If I don't get this right my career will be over."*

These are just a few examples from coachees from every profession including barristers, managers, surgeons, graphic departments, team leaders. Just about in every profession, individuals carry these thoughts and I have heard them all plus more, so many times.

IN MY COACHING, I challenge the thinking, break the 'self-imposed rules and assumptions' that are all self-created. Because the beliefs may need to be changed, I create a paradigm shift which is usually needed for change; I challenge the beliefs.

Coaching is perfect for this, and it is fantastic to break through some of these beliefs that are all self-created by many of us, sadly mostly negative beliefs. I will always create a safe place for coaching to take place and everything discussed is entirely confidential. You can do this yourself by challenging your beliefs.

THERE IS a cycle and people will often fall into this trap. That is when faced with a tough situation (the adversity) we create a belief (usually negative), then the consequence is negative. You can change that cycle if you choose to do so, face the adversity, create a positive belief then the result is positive.

The problem sometimes is that when you think it, then you believe it, and sadly you then start to act it. It is this cycle that if we are not careful, we fall into a self-fulfilling prophecy. I think as a starter you can start to think about your life and what you would like to change. Then I think a good thing to do is how have you dealt with adversity before, and how resilient are you already, how strong are you.

A fantastic thing to do is to look at yourself and reflect on areas from the past, why you are the person you are. Think about times in your life that you have had to deal with adversity. What did you do about it? Writing helps, it always helps to put your thoughts down on paper. But it is essential that you think and write about the positive times, not the negative. Think about one key area and what you did about it. Dealing with adversity in life, we all have to deal with it; it is what grows us and develops us. Essential to understand how we have dealt with it in the past and how we have set our habits up to deal with it.

Dealing with adversity can be a positive and encouraging experience. It can lead to huge growth and development if you take the learning from it. Sadly, people don't see it this way; they see it as people are out to get them, they feel the victim, and everyone else is seen as the persecutor. This is set up in your mind and probably not true it is how your inner critic is leading you.

Adversity can be severe, it teaches us lessons through life, but it moves us forward, we grow through adversity, it just sometimes hurts us in the process. I think we have to take the positive from our situations, and that is the crucial point when faced with tough situations. Remember writing your thoughts down does help; it will show you where your brain goes and then you can change it. Sometimes once you see visually where your brain goes it will give you the evidence you may need to show how you think.

When something bothers us, or we become anxious about something, we waste an awful amount of energy focusing on this. What a waste of time and energy or worrying about a mistake. The focus can be unbalanced, and generally, people are focused on the negative aspects of their life and not the positive. Negativity works 100% of the time, so why waste time on it?

ASK YOURSELF EMPOWERING QUESTIONS SUCH AS "WHAT COULD I DO DIFFERENTLY".

WHY WASTE ENERGY ON SOMETHING NEGATIVE?

I recently had a coachee who had struggled with an exam result when all of her training had gone exceptionally well. The rant for at least 20 mins was about the one error she made; there was not one mention of the endless hours of good work and preparation that had been done.

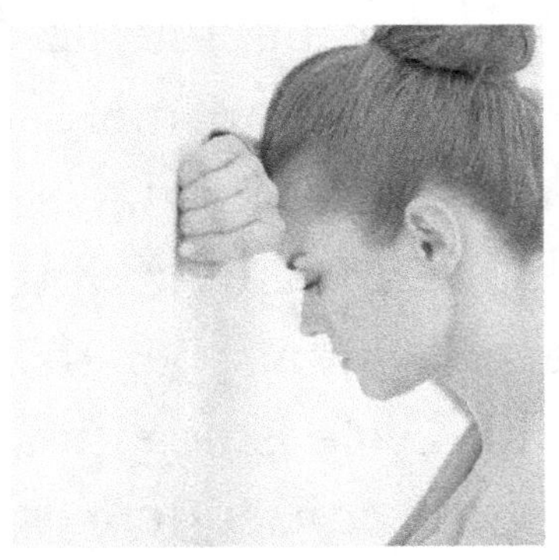

As I sat watching her, the focus and energy wasted on the mistake seemed ridiculous. I did wonder why she, along with the majority of peo-ple, could not have channelled this much energy in a much more beneficial way.

MAKE A MISTAKE, but don't let it take your focus. Recognise the error then take the lesson from it. When in this situation reflect on why the mistake happened, then think about the situation again. But this time, think about the situation and how you would deal with it differently. Always remember that mistakes need to be looked at positively, because this is where the learning takes place. If you don't make mistakes, sadly this does not build the database which is our brain. So why waste endless energy on something you are not comfortable with? Take the learning and stay positive.

AS MENTIONED PREVIOUSLY, when people face adversity, the beliefs that come and play on minds (which of course takes capacity) are dreadful, e.g. "I am not good enough", "I look like an idiot", "I am going to be found out". Adversity equals beliefs, which equal consequences. If this cycle is negative what a waste of time and energy, the consequences will always be negative. I would always suggest that when you face adversity, you see the positives; then the outcomes will be positive. It is the patterns in our brain, so stay with the positive, learn from the mistakes but focus your energy down the right routes.

ENERGY PLAYS SUCH a massive part in our learning; it is how you focus this that gets results. We naturally waste energy on negativity; it is a pattern set up when we are young. The brain will only know to follow that route unless you change it and create a new pathway. So I always encourage positively using energy and again if you make mistakes see this as a positive, not a negative.

NEGATIVE THINKING WORKS **100%** OF THE TIME.

6

HAVE YOU WRITTEN YOUR NEXT CHAPTER?

All of us have a book to write, and we could all write plenty of chapters. What a great experience to do this to find how your journey has evolved and where you are today.

THERE WILL BE highs and lows, but overall the positive from it needs to be congratulated. Think about how much success you have had in life, the joys of living on this planet both at home and work. Just doing something is a success in life.

Then where do you go next, because your book is only partially written? How would you write on those blank pages, where do you want the journey to go, what would you like to see? I think in life we hit 'stuck areas', and on those 'stuck areas', we make choices that are sometimes forced. Some are in a direction that improves us, some maybe not, but they are all a direction from being stuck or wanting change. Have you recognised that feeling, feeling stuck on something not knowing what to do next? I think this is a great time to sit with not knowing and see what pops up when you stare at the blank pages. There will be something, recognise what you notice and choose your destiny. Don't let it just happen.

I would suggest that you start your book or diary and then sit with the blank pages. Think about what you would like to see on those pages.

Just sit with that for a moment and imagine, visualise what you would like to see on them. Take control of your next direction; don't just let things happen, make what you want to happen, happen. You choose your future and destiny. You can create anything if you decide to. I often hear those comments from people, "I'm still here", as they go into work and I do wonder why people don't take more control in their life to change.

Always ask yourself what have you missed so far in your life? Is there anything you desperately wanted to change whether small or large but still procrastinate with it. Write that chapter, that will be an excellent chapter to self explore.

So, go ahead, write your next chapter, write what you would like to see, imagine, create the next stages of your life. Don't let things happen and make the direction for you, create your path, be in control and start to write your next chapter. You can change your life in an instant, if you want to.

To start your next chapter in life, you just need to turn the page and create the change.

7

WHAT WOULD MAKE A HUGE DIFFERENCE IN YOUR LIFE, IF YOU WENT TO WORK ON IT?

Have you ever thought to yourself what do I want to change, really change, then actually address it?

THE BIGGEST FAILURE with a lot of people is holding themselves back. This then means never really working in an area you want to change, just accepting things as they are. Sometimes little changes make significant progress over time rather than one major difference. Small changes are a way forward.

Think about it, what would you like to change, why and how could you do things differently.

Grade yourself and think why you have given yourself the grade? Whether you have given yourself numbers on the scale 0-10 or A, B, C ask yourself why? And then where would you like it to be.

Then the hard work begins with what little changes you can make yourself. Sometimes coaching is required so that thinking is done differently, challenged. What do you want to be different, your overall goal? We all have deep desires and that we want to achieve, and we can all achieve. Sometimes to accomplish through some help from a coach on the side is what can help and improve you. Expectations vs reality may creep into your thinking. Expectations can sometimes be unrealistic which is why little steps are better than one huge one. It is about starting to get to work on the change. Being proactive and not fearing mistakes and failure.

YES, there are a couple of areas that do hold us back, that fear of failure and what others may think, the thought that you think someone else may think you are stupid. Fear of failure is all in our minds, our self-imposed rules which sometimes need to be targeted for change but can be done if we want to change something. It is about being good enough and excepting it. Really start to think about a change you want to work on then start questioning your thinking, where you see yourself and where you want to be, the result. Then start working in little areas. Keep the mindset to create change and make the changes but keep them small. Always keep the end goal in sight, and you will be successful.

ALL IS REQUIRED IS SMALL STEPS, FOR CHANGE YOU JUST NEED TO TAKE THE NEXT ONE.

8

GET COMFORTABLE WITH BEING UNCOMFORTABLE

If you want to make progress or significant changes in life, then get comfortable with being uncomfortable. I feel that this is linked with stepping out of your comfort zone because being uncomfortable is good for you; it can help you develop in life.

MY BACKGROUND TAUGHT me that it was important to be slightly nervous before controlling an aircraft, it is the same for pilots or any job where there is pressure.

That feeling you respond to just before you are placed in that uncomfortable position, what happens with that feeling? Before that feeling becomes second nature in your line of work, it is a point for losing some capacity due to your nerves. I personally used to have a little trip to the restroom to have the nervous pee before controlling live aircraft. The release of adrenalin needed to make me alert. That was me getting ready and building myself up before going on the console.

Throughout all of my training environment, I always had that feeling, but I remember some great words from one of my old trainers from the 1980s. He said, "The day you stop having that feeling is the day you stop controlling", that was so true. This was the same when I learnt to fly, that uncomfortable feeling before I step into the plane, if I don't get it then I don't fly. Through life it is about getting comfortable with that feeling you don't like, this then can become normal, in my experience, it is so true, as when I am uncomfortable, it just feels normal. Bizarre really, it is so important though because that is how you will grow.

LIFE IS SO exciting when you look back and reflect. At times you don't realise that some of the significant changes in your life have come from some feelings or a trigger, not words. Think about what you see about yourself, recognise what is happening in you and learn to get comfortable with it. Coaching can help and guide the process, and usually other points come out during the journey, it is hugely beneficial. I personally really like the feeling of being uncomfortable, it makes me move forward in life. I always look for it so that I can overcome it, I love the challenge. This feels normal to me as I have created that pattern. You can create any pattern you want; you have to want to do it. I genuinely look for the uncomfortable feeling; it feels normal now.

THE MORE OFTEN YOU FEEL UNCOMFORTABLE, THE MORE IT BECOMES NORMAL.

9

EVER THOUGHT ABOUT HAVING A WHOLE DAY OF POSITIVITY?

The media is very much responsible for how we communicate. All we do these days is grab our phones, read the updated messages from social media and focus on what they want us to think. To get a feeling of what's happening these days, you have to read everything.

BUT WHAT IS it we read? Everything is negative, no matter where you go to read you learn so much negative information. The problem these days is that we continuously turn to our phones and laptops. So we read more negativity and are constantly bombarded with doom and gloom.

Can you imagine a whole day of reading just positive information? Imagine and visualise that type of day. Imagine all the media agreeing to have a full day of greatness. Just imagine what that feeling would be like what transference people would share with each other. It would be so incredibly powerful and positive, just amazing.

I believe it would be like the sun shining, that day when everyone wants to say good morning. Not like the day where the clouds are black, and everyone cannot be bothered to say hello.

What a thought that would be? I think we should start a campaign for this to happen to watch and witness the moods in everyone. A campaign for a paradigm shift for a day, to think about news differently. What a day that would be. This thought is already motivating me.

IF THIS POSITIVE article is motivating me, how many others are starting to feel motivated? A pure focus on positivity, it is an amazing experience and guess what? IT WORKS. It can change the way you think.

How often do you walk away from work, frustrated and disappointed because the day has not gone as planned? Do you ever reflect on the day and ask yourself what has happened through the day? What was good and what would you like to be different, what would you change.

CLOSE YOUR EYES EVERY DAY AND SMILE FOR ONE MINUTE. THE REALITY IS, WE HAVE A LOT TO BE POSITIVE ABOUT.

10

WHAT IS A PERFECT DAY?

Sometimes in our lives, we have such expectations from what we expect out of the day. The problem is that we create such self-imposed rules on ourselves and our workplaces that all we do is build our own disappointment.

OUR EXPECTATIONS versus realism are sometimes streets apart. We as human beings tend to focus on our frustrations from the day which can create negativity. This then creates the domino effect so that when we go home, we feel we have had such a rubbish day and it affects us mentally.

The first ***"How would I like the day to run"***, regardless of your profession, what is a perfect day.

Then follow this with ***"What were the limitations of the day"***, this can go in so many directions, really think about this.

Then say to yourself ***"How did my day go?"*** Use a journal, write it down and really push your thinking, break the day down.

Sometimes, if you work through these three questions, you bring the expectations back into realism. This will improve your overall thinking about the day. Then you may go home reflecting on the day in a much more positive way and ready to go back the next with a slightly different mind-set. If your expectations are so different to the real-ism, they can create negativity and will hinder your proactivity and motivation to go back for more.

OUR SELF-IMPOSED rules create problems because we can be very hard on ourselves.

This, in the long run, can create problems with your health and your willingness to move forward, even for another day at work. We do create our own rules; only we hear that voice in our head telling us what the day should be like. You can use these questions because they are such a fantastic cycle to separate the reality from expectations. You can use these personally in your life or work environment. Think about it, how do you manage, how do you supervise, how do you work, how do you think about your kids, it is so important to get the right balance? Remember changes begin in the mind, our own self-imposed rules need to be real to create the right belief systems and increase self-confidence.

COACHING IS fantastic for looking into these areas; coaching can create a different way of thinking and is the best place to work out our patterns. Changes begin in our minds, our minds with our own rules. Unless you are challenged how do you know what you don't know? Coaching is fantastic for challenging and encouraging coachees to think differently. When you think in a different way you learn something new.

CHANGE BEGINS IN OUR MINDS WITH OUR OWN RULES.

11

YOU DON'T KNOW WHAT YOU DON'T KNOW

Our brains don't always like change; they are happy to stay in one place, stay in our own personal comfort zone. It takes an input from a coach to guide them in a different direction so that the coachee can learn more.

COACHING IS an excellent place for this to happen, in fact, a perfect place for this to happen. A coach provides the space for the awareness in a coachee to grow and for this to happen.

A coach has to park their outside life and judgements to one side, to be in the room to listen to the coachee. We as human beings are entirely ignorant with our views on life. A lot of this is because, "We don't know what we don't know." Our opinions, biases and judgements are based on our world, which is very small in comparison to the broader world.

I enjoy watching the light bulb moment in a coachee, when a small comment from myself can suddenly create a shift in the way that the coachee thinks. Remember, the brain will fight change because it is comfortable with its own established habits. We build our habits throughout our lives, and it takes a lot of work to create new patterns and habits, the brain will always fall back on what it knows.

Our head is full of habits and patterns; this is where it is most comfortable. How difficult is it to create new habits, sometimes very hard so we choose not to do this? Pushing yourself to step out of your comfort zone is hard, forcing a new pattern is hard but you can always do it if you choose to do it.

Sometimes a coach can create that change for you by guiding a new habit, a change in the way you think. We as human beings are very set in our ways, and the brain does not like change unless we force that habit in, a habit of enjoying a change. What a fantastic difference in the way you can think if you choose to. We often tell ourselves we can't do things. Sometimes the way to deal with that is to do what you fear most first; ensure you force that habit. The tasks of the day; do we tend to leave the one we don't want to do till later, how about doing it first? Enjoy the feeling of completeness and the fact you dealt with it, force this new habit in yourself.

You can conquer anything if you choose to do it but think about yourself, where you are and what you notice in yourself. What do you do, ever reflected before? Have you looked at your habits? Such patterns can re-occur in life, throughout your life. Remember you don't have to stay with them, you can change them if you decide to do this then act on your decision to break your habit.

Habits are tremendous but create great ones, get rid of those you don't like about yourself and recreate a change. At the time of recognising you are about to do something which is an old habit, stop and think about your decision, you have a choice. The choice to change the direction or the opportunity to stay the same, what do you want? The more difficult choice although wanting it will be the change of the direction of travel. However, once made a few times you can slowly change that habit. Keep a record at the end of the day. See what choices have come up and the directions you have chosen. A useful exercise to look at what you think you have done, to what you have done.

IF YOU WANT SOMETHING YOU HAVE NEVER HAD, YOU HAVE TO DO SOMETHING YOU HAVE NEVER DONE.

12

WHY DO PEOPLE THINK THEY STRUGGLE WITH DECISION MAKING

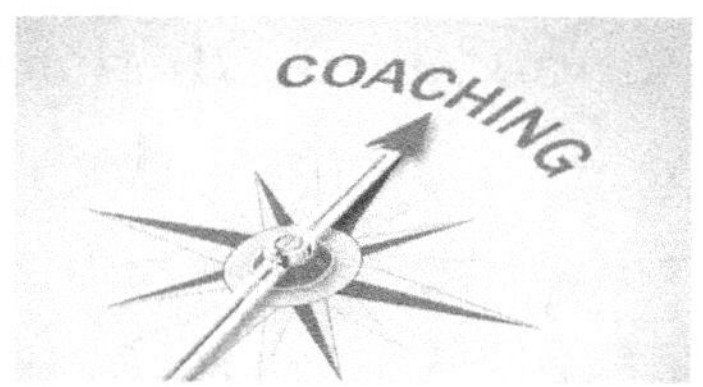

Decision making is such a significant area of life that some people tend to struggle. Procrastination is a common theme I hear which I always find interesting.

WHEN YOU THINK about this in a different way you realise that we make decisions all the time, the clothes we choose to dress in, driving to work, drinking water, coffee or tea, all day, all the time. What is the difference? Well the decisions you make without thinking about are all habits, habits that we are used to doing, or shall I say, what the brain is used to doing. When you sit and hover with decisions and tell yourself you can't make one, it is because your brain does not want to change. Your mind likes to be comfortable, in its comfort zone!

What can you do about it? Well I believe repetition, repetition, repetition is the answer. The best way is to form a new habit! It is not hard, it is about stepping out of that comfort zone and taking the risk, then do it again, then doing it again and again. All the time you will increase your decision-making process by creating new pathways in your brain to the point where you will have formed a new habit.

DECISION MAKING IS difficult when faced with huge consequences but any decision is better than none. Remember that life is a journey, and you make choices, and if you make one that is not the correct one for you, you make another. The key is to reflect on what positives have come from the choices that you make. The brain will automatically fall on the negative areas but the key is to push for the positive ones then realise the learning that has taken place for you and how you can take this forward.

DECISION MAKING IS EASY, at the point of choice say 5,4,3,2,1 then go... if you don't within 5 seconds your brain will talk you out of it. A typical example of this is, "Shall I ask the person in the local restaurant out for a date?" If you don't act straight away your inner voice will likely start to say, "They won't be interested in me." Your brain can be a problem for you if you let it and sadly you will never know if that person would have gone or not.

REMEMBER, YOU CAN CHANGE YOUR LIFE IN AN INSTANT, IF YOU REALLY WANT TO.

13

HOW DO YOU DEAL WITH THE ELEPHANT IN THE ROOM?

How often do you think about what is not being said in a conversation? I think this is such a huge area that people miss in a conversation let alone how to deal with it.

IN COACHING, when you are trained well, you learn to pay attention to your instinct. Just for a second think about how many times you have walked away thinking "They don't mean that", or "I wish I had said", I suspect probably lots of times. Furthermore, if you reflect a bit deeper, you will probably realise you have missed the key area in a conversation. This is so frustrating if you wish to support the other person, relationships being No 1 in both work and personal lives. It's the relationship that counts, and it's that which will make progress for someone.

COACHING IS all about this area, what is not being said. This area is hugely important in communication, 55% instinct against 7% words. Yet we all pay attention to the language unless taught otherwise. Why is this? What is it about your feelings you tend not to share? Additionally, not sharing what you notice? A lot of the times it is usually that you don't know to deal with this, how to question or intervene with this without offending.

How do you do this? How do you share something you are feeling or noticing or even sensing without alienating? I always say set the person up before you share what you notice. It literally is as easy as "Do you mind if I share" or "Do you mind if I tell you what I have noticed". This is also a great way to share the body language you notice. For example, leg kicking or foot tapping, eye contact, a shift in someone's body after a question. The timing is also important for the timing and balance of the intervention.

In my coaching, I tend to look for this as a priority. Sometimes I don't even listen to the story I stay focussed on my instincts, feelings, or body language. I have found this has been tremendously important for the breakthrough to get to another level with my clients. This is a skill that needs to be practised and one I really work on when delivering my coaching courses. We spend a lot of time working on this area in practice sessions with other delegates.

You have to notice yourself and the best way to do this is writing it all down.

14

___

WHAT IS SHAME?

Have you ever thought about what your shame is? We all carry shame in some way, for example, feeling embarrassed and guilty about something. Your belief system of not feeling good enough or others are better than you is not a nice feeling.

As a coach, you need to be aware when your client sat in front of you the shame they may carry. Shame is a horrible feeling, when you feel it, you feel bad and have some regret. Ask yourself how often do you feel this and what does this feel like.

Another question is, how often do you shame others? Do you notice yourself doing this, and what does this mean? Shame leads to depression and self-esteem and can be very lonely. Shame is a topic worth exploring in detail with your clients and yourself as a coach. Knowing your own shame helps you understand sitting in the client's shoes.

A good exercise is to ask yourself what your shame is then follow through with a journal. Really think about how you feel when you notice any feeling, and what feelings and thoughts trigger. it will be very uncomfortable but great learning if you write for five mins a day. As a coach, you will be used to reflecting your clients won't be.

Where does shame come from? It can come from various sources culture is one of them. Imagine the eighties where homosexuals and lesbians were made to feel ashamed because of their preferences. Think about what that must have felt like just because it was different. The feelings must have been huge. What did it do to those people, and some will still carry some shame. This will of course affect your self-esteem and the self-worth you place on yourself.

Finally, think about people from authority from your childhood like teachers and parents. A simple comment from them will play on your mind and lead to other factors in later life. Something like University is not for people like this.... Think about what that creates through life, that voice in your head.

Some people hide their shame, feel ashamed to show their shame. Think about if you hide it under something like anger. Serious shame leads to depression and self-harm.

What is your shame? Great reflection as a coach to recognise this yourself.

WE ALL CARRY SHAME - WE JUST DON'T LIKE TO ADMIT IT.

15

LOW SELF-ESTEEM IS DESTRUCTIVE

I think this is such a vast area that seems to be kept hidden in people's closets. Lots of people struggle with low self-esteem; it is a hindrance to many. So, what is it?

IT IS a subjective evaluation of your own worth. It creates self-beliefs that hold you back. Low self-esteem affects so many people and creates problems for so many individuals. It affects your performance, creates anxiety and creates negative thoughts. It really is huge.

Lots of beliefs are created in your mind when you carry low self-esteem, things like; I am not good enough, I am going to fail, they think I am not good enough, really self-destroying and very destructive for some people. This feeds that wonderful inner critic, the voice that so many of us know about these days, the voice that holds you back. But the good news is you can change this, yes you can.

I think it's such a good question to ask yourself where your self-esteem lies. High or Low, how high and how low? How do you rate yourself and value yourself? Think about your own beliefs and values? This will help you understand where your self-esteem may lie. I think a lot of us underestimate ourselves because we don't want to say we have lots of strengths. We don't feel comfortable saying we deserve something, good at something;

it feels strange saying this to yourself, giving your-self appreciation. For some reason, a lot of people will choose to dislike themselves and not like themselves, such a sad pattern in people.

I REALLY BELIEVE you can change your beliefs if you want to. You can change the negative beliefs to positive beliefs by accepting and making the decision to change. Think about it, you are as good as everyone else, and people are not out to get you. Love yourself, be happy with yourselves. When was the last time you told yourself you were proud of something you had done? Sadly, this will not be as much as you would have told yourself how useless you are.

WE HAVE one life and to hold yourself back and not make the most of your life is really very sad. But the good news is "You can do something about it". You can change, you can think differently once you create the habit to look for the change; this is the starting point.

Just pause for a second. Think about some of your strengths, don't go straight for your weaknesses, look at your strengths. Once you have done this look at them and think about how you can improve on these, so they become outstanding. You will be able to make strengths stronger. You just have not been taught how to do this.

WHETHER YOU THINK YOU CAN OR YOU THINK YOU CAN'T - YOU ARE RIGHT.

16

THE POWER OF DECISION MAKING

I recently made a decision that had been long coming but took a while to make. Once I made this and then acted on this, the feeling afterwards I cannot underestimate. The power of making the choice I made created a shift in my outlook.

THE FASCINATING THING is once this was made the avenues and roads just seemed to open up. My focus shifted and then looked at more possibilities that were open to me. The possibilities changed immediately, the choices that appeared were a lot more real than just thoughts in my head.

The reality is the majority of us stay in situations for too long, feeling stuck. We don't always know we are stuck until after the decision has been acted on. When you get better at decision making you will look forward to making them.

THE POWER of decision making can change so much in your life. I see so many clients who are clearly stuck in their life. Avoiding the fact, they need to make a decision, they may fear doing this because of something that may have happened to them in the past.

The common themes are relationships, organisations, and work. We get lost in the What If's, fearing making the move. The worst thing that can happen is to not make one, to sit on something fearing something that maybe not there.

Through life and every single day, we make decisions, we just don't think that we do. We have so many little habits made which have come from our decision making, we just seem to be unaware of this.

THE WORD DECISION comes from Latin and it literally means "to cut off". By making a decision we effectively cut out all other possibilities. We make them inaccessible. Remove them from the equation, they are no longer open to us. We must always move forward, don't let not making a decision hold you back, there is nothing to fear just opportunities to gain.

THERE IS ABSOLUTELY no doubt that we all have fantastic power, yes we can change our lives in an instant. What a tremendous feeling that is, to know that you can change your life in a split second and that no one can stop you, once you recognise this fact then you are on the road to truly sorting yourself out and taking control of your life.

The best thing of all is that this power comes free, we don't have to pay anything, it is within us all, we just need to recognise it, and of course, we have to put it into practice. We are, of course, talking about our power and ability to be able to make a decision.

We all have experiences of making decisions though, or not making them (that's another blog) I want you to fully experience the awesome power of what it is like to make one though and the massive benefits that can result.

OF COURSE, many of the decisions we make on a daily basis are really more of a 'preference' which is what you could call a weak decision or to be honest not actually making a decision at all which is exactly what will happen! We make preferences all the time, how many New Year's resolutions do we make such as "I want to lose weight" or "I want to stop smoking" they are preferences. You and I secretly know that when we say these words like that we don't actually mean it and sometimes we even know it when we are saying it! No surprise then when after a few weeks we are back to our old habits again. Also using disempowering words such as "I will try to.." if you ever have a party and someone says they will "try" to be there you can put them on the never turning up list! The word try is a very disempowering word as it gives us an option not to do it as we are only trying.

WHEN WE MAKE a real decision it is genuinely empowering and focused, like a powerful laser beam that can't be stopped, not that we can't change our decisions, that is important also but the beam has the power to burn through any element of doubt such as convenient excuses such as "I didn't have time" or "I couldn't because of ....." and "it will be ok just this once" not that there's anything wrong with saying these things, but in providing these excuses we didn't really make a decision. Also, by using these excuses, we can easily make breaking a decision a habit and the habit we want to have is regularly making decisions, real ones, not preferences.

Decisions can be an extremely positive influence; they improve self-esteem, and they enable us to take control of our lives, you just need to make one to find out. When was the last time you made one?

THERE'S ONLY WRONG WORSE THAN MAKING A BAD DECISION AND THAT IS NOT MAKING ONE!

17

CONFIDENCE

Confidence is such a vast area in all of us, have you ever reflected on how confident you are already, flipping it to a positive from a negative, thinking about it differently.

IN MY COACHING PRACTICE, confidence appears so often. I think sometimes people don't realise how confident they are already. The word confidence is interpreted in so many ways; people worry about what the word confidence means to them personally and how they think they should be. The word expectation always springs to mind, I think if people are perfectionists, this may cause some of the problems.

The first thing I always ask is "How confident are you already?"

Think about this and where you are confident. Then think about what has made you confident in these areas. You will have over life hit adversity in so many ways but never thought about how you have dealt with these areas in confident ways. A good exercise is to write down three areas that you have found confidence, just take a few seconds to do this. Then reflect on what you have written. Just noticing the words, those words will have significant meaning to you.

What is Self Confidence? The three drivers of

Self Confidence are 1) Confidence in others, 2) Confidence in one's own capabilities, and 3) Confidence in life. This is where it all starts; Self Confidence is central to our existence, we don't study it, we observe it and then watch it grow. But we must nurture it and grow it wisely.

We all have confidence, but it's things in life that take control of it. The negative thoughts we carry can hurt it and of course, our self-esteem too. This then gives us problems when dealing with adversity, and before long, we tell ourselves we are not good enough. We say it, we then believe it but sadly, we then act on it.

To have confidence in ourselves is to know how you can handle the unexpected, not to mistakenly believe that life is foreseeable. There are times when there are situations where competence is needed, this is where confidence is not needed, that's because you have probably dealt with the specifics a thousand times, be careful not to mix them up.

SELF-ESTEEM CAN BE A PROBLEM, a lot of this is from early experiences. For example, punishment, neglect, failing to meet parental standards, failing to meet peer group standards, as an absence of good things (praise, affection, warmth and interest), being the odd one out at home or school, all have a factor in self-esteem and confidence.

How do I change and start to think differently? Little changes are key. Every day write down one thing that you are confident with and one thing you wish you had acted differently on. It is the little changes you need to start the change.

DURING COACHING, I think it is useful to run this exercise as so much can come from it. Until you really pay attention to this area you don't know. We all in life are slightly cautious and under-confident at times; that is life. Confidence grows through repetition but stepping out of your comfort zone is key to growing your confidence. If you don't try, you will never move forward. So many of us hold back due to fear of failure or how others will think of us.

So where would you scale your confidence levels look at both within yourself personally and then with your work? Then look at how you see yourself. Ask the question, "What would I like to be different?" and What could I do differently?". Look at yourself and how you see yourself, don't compare yourself to others look at you. You will miss the qualities you do have thinking you need to be someone else.

ONE THING THAT IS CERTAIN, CONFIDENCE CAN BE GROWN AND DEVELOPED.

18

WHAT WOULD YOU LEAST LIKE OTHERS TO KNOW ABOUT YOU

When you look at yourself, really look at yourself a good question to ask is "What I don't want to write about" This is a beneficial exercise to do as a coach. To recognise some areas in yourself, you would least like your client to know about.

IT IS A REALLY strange feeling to admit your faults, but as a coach, you do become used to sharing your innermost thoughts and feelings with peers. I always think you need to remind yourself of your vulnerability before a session with a client. Those feelings you carry are in everyone.

It is very useful to think about the areas you keep hidden, the imposter, the inner critic, thinking about the words that hold you back that trigger in a flash. Those moments you would prefer not to remember, but then the key is to flip it and recognise those are the times that made you who you are. We are all unique, but we must know ourselves and pay attention to the areas we prefer to not acknowledge as readily as our stronger areas, the areas we like about ourselves.

As a coach, we must remember the client, that immense feeling they feel when they walk into the room, and how much vulnerability they will be feeling. They will be holding so much that they would prefer to keep hidden. That is why it is so important that you the coach create a safe space, this is so important for the client to share their most secretive areas, the areas they prefer to keep hidden.

Through my practice, I think those first few minutes are vital to building the chemistry together, the rapport, confidentiality, the safe space to show vulnerability, the comfortable feeling you need in a coaching session.

Try the exercise, "What would I least like my clients to know about me", really useful for you to remember those areas within yourself that you push to one side. They may be triggered in a session with a client, recognise these, and just how they make you feel. Think about the anxiety that your client may feel and the triggers that will happen for them. As a coach, you have to come alongside the client, sit in their shoes.

This is a simple chapter to help you remember who you are and to think about the areas you prefer to not show, very useful but incredibly powerful and can create so much change when you face them.

ADMISSION OF A VULNERABILITY IS A STRENGTH NOT A WEAKNESS.

ARE YOU STUCK?

Stuck in life, that routine you do every day, those words "still here, Monday morning feeling" I often hear words like that in my clients. What about your personal life, stuck there, same house, same walks, same shops? Sometimes you must ask yourself "Why do I continue to do the same things when I would like to change them?"

I FIND it interesting that lots of people fall back into their habits and routines after they use words like, "I have had a great holiday or a great break". Then they fall back into their stuck lives? back to the same routine. Guess what, it does not have to be that way, being stuck is choice. Sometimes people don't realise they are stuck they just moan, others know they are stuck but choose not to do anything about it.

You can change your life if you choose to, break the routine and stuckness. Bring your holidays and great weekend breaks to work. Change the routine, even plan to change the routine, planning is better than doing nothing. Life is so short, and there are so many opportunities out there, but people fear them, fear doing something different. Furthermore, they don't know what they don't know. Life is exciting, it is about realising where you are personally and doing something about it.

When you look at yourself, I mean really look at yourself what do you notice? Where are you energised, where are you stuck, and what would you like to be different? Then when you write these thoughts down, you can start to see your patterns, where the stuckness lies. Then think about what little changes you can make, remember little changes lead to big moves, but the process needs to get going.

Do you find yourself stuck in life? One of those questions you sometimes have to ask yourself as you face the day to day routine with no change. Some of us like this, the majority don't, so why is this? Ask yourself the question what would you like to be different?

Look at three areas in your life, **career, life, and relationship** and break them down to see if you think change is needed. Ask yourself a question, what is important to you? Look at your values and what you would really like.

When it comes to change do you feel you need to resist this? Is it the uncertainty that holds you back or do you have fear with change? Sometimes this happens due to circumstances that you may have had in your life before.

THE KEY IS TO START, make a decision and start the process then once you do this you will be starting the change. Look at the three areas and give yourself a goal in each of them, remember this will be a long-term goal. Then start the process making little changes to move towards your goal.

THIS IS where I believe journals are fantastic to push and drive the change, forcing yourself. Writing allows you to see the changes happening, writing every day works. This forces in new behaviour, it makes you look at the words you have written to see if anything else jumps out. Sometimes you will write the same words, is this stuckness again? Then look for what you could do differently, it really is fantastic because it creates creativity.

Feel confident, don't let the inner critic hold you back, you can achieve anything in life if you choose to do this.

Stuck in the stuckness I always say, do something about it, energise your life and make everyday fun, every day there can be little changes. I am fortunate that I don't worry, I make decisions, then make another one if I am not happy. One thing I have is the habit to change something when I recognise I need to do something different.

The change is incredibly rewarding, which is why I don't mind making changes. It is so important to recognise in your life where you are, do you want to make your house your last one before you leave this planet? Is this the last job you are going to have, are you happy and content?

These are huge areas to change it's the little changes that improve these. Remember **you don't know what you don't know**, look for some change it is very powerful and incredibly rewarding. Coaching significantly helps this process.

RECOGNITION OF BEING STUCK IS A SIGNIFICANT STEP TO MOVING FORWARD.

20

WHAT IS COACHING CULTURE?

Having quite a lot of experience coaching, supervising and mentoring the biggest mistake I see with people is in the understanding of what coaching is. I am a firm believer coaching takes time to understand and master, a seriously long time. It is not about tick box coaching, in other words coaching by numbers just like painting like numbers. Coaching is much more than that.

ON MY COURSES the first thing I say at the beginning of any course is I will not be able to make you a coach in two days as an example, it is just not going to happen. The companies that say you can be a coach with some written work, no monitoring of your sessions and giving you feedback on written work do not turn you into a coach. It is practice and understanding, receiving feedback on the practical sessions on all the data that is in the room. It is about understanding what is not being said and sharing this.

What I do on any of my courses is to give you some skills and techniques to start the process to understand what the coaching culture is. Coaching is a fantastic skill to have and use in all aspects of your life. Whether you use it professionally or at home with partners kids, the skills work everywhere.

80 per cent of the workforce who have experienced coaching say it positively impacts their work performance, productivity, communication skills,

and well-being, 65 per cent of those in a coaching culture are highly engaged, only 36 per cent of organisations offer coaching-specific training

In addition to engagement, coaching also improves business performance. A recent Bersin & Associates study reports that providing managers with coaching skills can provide 130% in business performance.

Consider the following benefits of a coaching culture, and you won't have to wonder why your company needs it; you'll be wondering why everyone's not doing it.

Engagement leads to higher levels of productivity, creativity, profitability, and employee retention.

Coaching makes employees feel valued and improves job and career satisfaction. But a coaching culture achieves those goals and goes far beyond individual employee satisfaction by creating and supporting optimal people and business performance.

Coaching comes into the picture, employees feel more engaged and more valued, and experience higher productivity and produce strong bottom-line results. Executive coaching, performance coaching, and coaching for development all play different roles in a coaching culture, but all create stronger bonds and forge better working relationships that support business goals and performance.

Coaching routines, coaching training, and management accountability for coaching are just a few ways to begin building coaching into your culture.

ADOPTING A COACHING CULTURE IN YOURSELF IS WHAT PERSONAL DEVELOPMENT IS ALL ABOUT.

21

___

STAYING SILENT & NOTICING

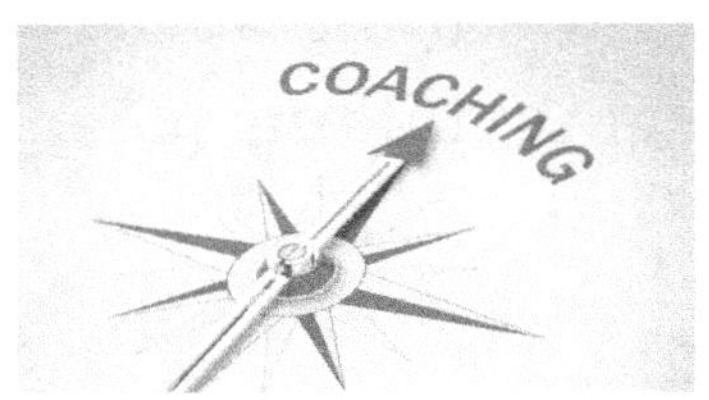

How often do you stay silent and notice? Think about it "really notice". Coaching is a fantastic process for individuals to improve in any area of their life, both professionally and personally.

I HAVE FOUND since mastering my coaching skills; staying silent can be an incredible experience. I genuinely love to see the change in individuals as they move between recognition and awareness of thoughts and feelings.

Watching people has become a habit of mine. Years ago, I would have jumped in with my own opinions and my thoughts. Not now, I learn so much more watching, noticing and listening. Even if I have a prejudgement on someone's views, I still sit. It is a habit I have formed.

In life, we experience so much, and when we have time with both work colleagues and friends, we gain an opinion on our conversations. The problem is it is very easy to try to force opinion in a conversation. This, of course, means you stay in the same direction and don't listen to understand someone else's point of view, still stuck on your own. Most fall into the trap of twisting what you hear to fit!

As I write this the current situation with our election is a nightmare! All I hear are peoples own personal points of view and of course we all vote based on our own experiences and our own inter-ruption of the world. This is where I have noticed over the last few weeks people making judgements based on what has been their opinion and no matter what they hear, they still respond based on their already decided judgements. It has been so interesting, observing and noticing regardless of what side you sit.

This is so sad, that means we don't listen to un-derstand. The majority of people seem to be about juggling their words to fit their opinions and judgements on what they hear. Listening and noticing is a far greater skill to gain and very powerful. If you do this, you are then in a much better place to offer something more valuable and unlikely to create any resentment or a bad feeling.

If you fancy creating a new habit and wish to learn, understand and practice this powerful skill, then come to learn properly. This is a great skill, and you don't know when this skill is good as you have nothing to compare it to. You don't know what you don't know, and it is hard to get the right opinion if you are not told otherwise.

Staying silent and noticing is a massive skill; not everyone has this perfected, and I would advise everyone to learn this excellent coaching technique.

SILENCE AND REFLECTION IS POWERFUL TOOL.

22

DO YOU EVER REFLECT ON HOW SOMEONE GREETS YOU?

Whenever I coach, I have always kept a record on how I am greeted. It is interesting to observe what you notice by both the person who greets you and how you react by the greeting.

SOMETIMES THERE ARE masses of energy, sometimes not, how does that affect you, what judgements do you create from this and how does this change you as a coach? What if you don't notice? I find it interesting when someone runs towards you, what does that say. When the person is genuinely reaching out to you, who do you represent to them? Are you someone that they have never had before or you remind them of someone? I recently had a client who did this, and what was interesting was how I responded.

This was a real child reacting to a parent, the role I probably played subconsciously, the fact I became the rescuer while this person was a victim. But how this made me feel and respond to how I responded to another client was different. Would I notice this as much if I did not reflect?

A different example and contrast are when I have felt a surge of energy run towards me, almost drowning me with enthusiasm. These are just two examples of the differences that I could have reacted massively different if I was not aware of. I noticed that I felt I wanted to question and listen differently. The way I am is always professional, but I did feel the differences and had to be careful not to show this in the sessions and stay fully present. It is essential to notice 'you' because this can create changes in the relationship that sits in the room.

I really would advise in doing this, really notice the reactions between you and your client even down to the tone in your voice and how you choose to guide the journey for the client.

Fascinating noticing 'you' but very important you separate what I would say is your own baggage, so you give your client 100% attention. Your world is different to the client, so in a coaching session, you must show nothing, so the client does not change with what they notice in you because they will but not be conscious like yourself as a coach.

SOMETIMES IT'S THE THINGS YOU NOTICE MORE THAN THE THINGS YOU HEAR THAT SAY THE MOST.

WHAT IS REFLECTION?

How often do you reflect on your day? Both, what went well and what could have been better. Reflection, I believe is one of the most rewarding and positive things you can do regardless of which area you are involved in, whether Training, Coaching or Mentoring.

IF IT IS DONE CORRECTLY it can adjust the way that you think, create opportunities to learn and to help you think about things differently. It help's with continuous improvement, making you better at what you do. How many of us have left after delivering training or coaching and reflected on the day, I mean really reflected?

On my coaching courses, I teach the skills to really reflect, look at some key areas and how to use them. Sometimes we will say we were good at something but then never think about why we were good and what was different to make us good? Reflection I believe is where the best learning takes place. It is a continuous cycle to reflect, and then move what you have learnt about yourself forward into the preparation for your next session. You can constantly strive to improve, reflection is the key.

You have to be committed, create a habit, remember when you are honest about making mistakes, you soon realise they are actually opportunities to learn, nothing to hide from, mistakes are important. Reflection helps you understand your mistakes, if you don't do this you will never learn and move forward. Mistakes are opportunities to learn because they create creativity! With reflection, you will learn about how your focus may be, how this affects your mood and performance and where your strengths are. It is all about the ability to continue to learn and grow.

A fantastic question for everyone to think

about. When was the last time you reflected on your working day? If you are brutally honest with yourself, I suspect not very often. I do hear the word 'rarely' a lot when I am coaching, the most common word I hear from coachees when I ask this question. Why is this? Are we working at our best at work, are there no minor changes you can make to improve your practice?

WORK for the majority is routine, go to work do your job and leave. Does it have to be this way? If you are not driven, why not, how about making yourself feel better, taking more ownership. This, in turn, helps self-esteem and confidence. Think about your working day daily, think what was good through the day, why and what did not go so well. What would you like to change, why and how? What is the purpose of you being there? Sometimes it is good to have the purpose for the day, week and month, always have a long-term goal and look at the small steps you can make for changes.

Reflection on your work is excellent, it is about forcing a pattern to your head. The pattern then gets formed, then a new habit is created and this then becomes normal. If you need to force yourself to do this because you may lack the action in yourself, then it is a good idea to have a coach on the side to do this, to encourage you.

Reflection is great, develop the pattern, keep a diary, write a couple of things down on an evening both positive and areas you wish to change and watch the process build. The key then, after reflection is to do something about it, take action.

Reflection is such a huge area and is by far a key area in life whether professionally or personally that can make such a difference.

NOT EVERYONE CAN BE THE BEST, IT IS ALL ABOUT BEING THE BEST YOU CAN BE.

24

THOSE WORDS 'HURRY UP'

When my mum used the words "Hurry up" to me, then the words "Get ready for school hurry up hurry up" Little did she know what patterns this would set up in me. Hurry up is just one of the five Kahler drivers but I relate very well to this one as I see it in everything that I do and one area I have to manage in myself especially when coaching.

I ALWAYS WORK FAST. I love juggling lots of tasks to work with, then complain about how much time I don't have. Then when I get the clear time what stress this can cause for me? Such a strange pattern. When we tell our children to hurry up what we fail to do is to say when not to hurry up, this can cause such an imbalance.

There are five drivers I am just focusing on this one as it resonates with me in everything I do. I always have to consider this when I am coaching, and I have had to learn to deal with this in my coaching sessions. Easy now but at first quite hard to separate my drivers and me from the coachees.

Years ago, I would in my head be continually watching the clock, tapping my fingers or feet if things were not moving quickly. I like to work quickly on tasks; this is all part of my makeup. Have you ever thought what your drivers are and how you deal with them and how to contain them? Think about yourself, or your staff and your coachees, are they consciously aware of their drivers. The patterns they may have and how they may be seen?

I used to use and hear the words "What a waste of a day" I don't like lots of thinking time, I like to be active all day. I have struggled to relax in the past because I am all about speed efficiency because of those words "Hurry up". Fantastic reflecting on you and the five drivers and how others may see this and why you are the way you are, the key, it is all about managing them.

In a coaching room, I must hold myself back when I feel the excitement from one of my coachees when they say something that triggers my instinct that they have this driver. It usually creates the picture of the story about the hare and the tortoise. Just reflect on that one for a second and recognise in yourself what jumps out in you? Is this in you or do you see it in one of your staff? Think about what is happening at the moment when you recognise this and what you can (if you choose to) do about it. Understanding the different stress areas from this driver is essential as with all the other Kahler drivers.

REMEMBER ALWAYS BE AWARE OF YOUR DRIVERS AND HOW THEY MAY AFFECT PEOPLE AROUND YOU.

25

IT'S ALL ABOUT HOW WE TAKE INFORMATION IN

Have you ever walked away from a meeting thinking you have agreed on something, then what you haven't agreed starts to happen? It is all about how we take our information in.

SOME OF US LIKE FACTS, really enjoy facts and need them to hang on to. Then there are others who find facts restrict their thinking; the facts get in the way. They can see better ways of doing things. Some people like them for evidence, others don't. Ask yourself a couple of questions, what do you do, do you rely on facts or do you think in a more inspirational way? Yes, you will do both but what do you do first.

A useful exercise in understanding yourself and why you may clash with others is to work out what your preference may be. Look at the picture you see in this blog and think about what you see first, colours, shapes, pictures or go straight to the artist or is it oil based or put a bigger picture to it? A useful exercise to see how different people around you are and what they see. No one way is the right way, and you don't want everyone to be the same, organisations need the mix.

However, what you need to be aware of is how it can come across. I recently had some time with a very bright young lad, clearly an Oxbridge individual with the way he thought outside the box on everything, great to work with him. I suggested he would need to be careful because some people around him will not always follow his thinking and will find him very vague and hard to understand. He had no idea and was shocked when with a few simple exercises he realised how different people were. He had a lightbulb moment when we were discussing this. He realised that this was why people did not always do what he thought they had agreed on. "How fascinating," He said, that is why some people appear negative to him, he actually said this. Some of his colleagues are likely to be practical, like experience and probably very matter of fact. This is what may appear negative as they can't see all the creative ideas working. The skill is having everyone working together and the practical people following up on the creative ideas, well the realistic ones, the ones the factual people can see working.

The key to understand from this is how different we take our information in and how frustrated we can be within our workplace where we see negativity, creativity, vagueness and direction. Remember people will see things very differently. Ask yourself, how do I take my information in, how am I seen?

JUDGE YOUR LEVEL OF COMMUNICATION BY THE RESPONSE YOU GET.

26

WHERE IS YOUR PERSONAL PERFECT PLACE TO GO?

As I sit and reflect on the year, it's only November and yes I know it is early but I do like to do this. Where is your place to go to really reflect personally?

MY FAVOURITE SPOT is by the pool in my wonderful home in Florida. But the place is more than what it reads. It is my personal tranquil place where I always think about when I am faced with the adversity of any sort. Not only when I face adversity also when I am not in the greatest of moods or feel low about something or myself. Let's face it we all go there from time to time but where do you think about it and what triggers you to climb out of it.

My place is here, in the villa by the pool, this is where I visualise, just sitting here now is no different to when I visualise this special place when I am at home or work in the UK. The smell of the air, the pool, the greenery lovely freshly cut grass and watching the wildlife that appears from time to time. I think about all of this, the beautiful special mornings of just sitting after my run or walk. I visualise all of this plus more.

The most significant part for me is the listening personally, the water sound that trickles around the area. There is a little run of water that runs between the Spa and pool, and I always listen for this. For those who don't visualise this may sound crazy, but it is not, it works. It is about creating the perfect place for you, the one place that you can hold internally to yourself.

That one place that creates such happy thoughts, using all of your senses, the sounds, the smells the visual snapshot you create. I love the feeling that comes from this, that special feeling that I feel run through my body as I feel so calm and comfortable. This is my place, this place works for me, and I can recall it at any time, and I do quite often when uncomfortable or in the face of adversity.

What is your place, where do you go? Do you go anywhere? Have you tried this? I can honestly say it is amazing and works fantastically well for calmness when at those times in life you need it. Whenever we feel those doubtful moments, the key is creation, the visualisation of the most wonderful place that fits your internal world. That very special place you can create in snapshot seconds that instantly creates a positive and fantastic feeling. Your own thoughts that can create feelings is where you can go if you choose to. It is about wanting to go there. Choosing too is a decision to be made and one that only you can take up.

PERFECT PLACE = CALM

27

POSITIVE MENTAL ATTITUDE

What is a positive mental attitude? There is a recurring theme in life that if you have a more positive mental attitude that you will be more successful, healthy, happier, and have more energy to deal with the adversity that life throws at you.

FROM MY PERFORMANCE COACHING BACKGROUND, this is a mindset I have helped and guided others to create, including myself a few years ago. It is about adopting new habits, getting rid of the negative ones, and making new changes in your life that will help you. Think about what you do at the point of adversity? Do you notice if you slump back or do you see it as an opportunity to create a shift in your way of thinking and turning it into a positive, being constructive instead of it being a criticism?

We spend our life's in the negativity and negativity works 100% of the time. The key is to deal with situations differently. Attitude is such a huge part in life and creating a proactive, positive mindset over a negative reactive one, works wonders.

How many times in a day do you look at your strengths, really focus on what you have done well? I suspect very rarely; we tend to focus on the negatives and why we can't do something. In a lot of my coaching sessions, I hear the recurring theme of why someone can't do something? I always suggest thinking about this in a different way to reasons why we can do something. If you think you can do something, you will do it.

Having a positive mental attitude leads to being more open to suggestions and encourages you to act on things rather than avoiding and making excuses. This means you are happier, and you will be able to deal with more stressful situations, becoming much more resilient.

Think about your first part of the day, something positive creates a powerful mindset for the day. Whatever suits you, but a positive start is better than a negative one. Start focusing on yourself and write things down, really interesting to see how you write about yourself and how much of a struggle it is to write positive points.

NEGATIVE THINKING WORKS **100%** OF THE TIME.

28

HAVING A GRATITUDE ATTITUDE

In my coaching and supervision sessions, I hear so much negativity. I do like to shift the paradigm sometimes and ask for the positives if the situation allows this to happen. It seems strange to my clients when I ask a simple question like "What have you got to be grateful for"?

IN LIFE, we have plenty to be positive about; it is hugely important in having a gratitude attitude. People find being negative so easy but being thankful seems slightly alien, and when asked what you have got to be happy and grateful for I am met with surprise. If you would like to do something about it, guess what you can!

Here is an exercise; ask yourself how happy you are and really think about the positives in your life, there will be plenty. We don't tend to focus on the areas we can be happy and grateful for it is all about what we don't like. If you have a positive mindset and you say to yourself every day what you have to be happy and grateful, you will start to build the habit of positivity. This is incredibly powerful and works.

A gratitude attitude creates greater happiness and positive emotions. This leads you to be able to deal with adversity better, and you will receive more enjoyable experiences in your life. It is proven you sleep better and build stronger relationships. A gratitude attitude is very powerful, the key is about adopting one, which everybody can.

A mindset of gratitude makes people feel more alive and in tune with themselves. This leads to better health and overall in tune with others. Why would you not want to create this?

HOW DO YOU CREATE THIS? A journal is a fantastic resource to use. All you have to do is write for five minutes a day either at the beginning of the day or the end or both if you choose to. This encourages you to think about the positives in your life, e.g. not it's raining again but how happy and grateful I am to feel and smell the rain, what a blessing. In our journals, it simply encourages you to think about what you do and then how you can think differently. It encourages humour and how much you can appreciate yourself and others. This is all perfect to think about what you have and not what you don't have.

START EACH DAY WHAT YOU ARE HAPPY AND GRATEFUL FOR.

29

REFLECTING ON YOUR USE OF COPING STRATEGIES

What does coping mean? I often hear in my coaching sessions from my clients that they are coping. I always think about what the word coping means to them. I think some people may not even know or realise they are using coping strategies/mechanisms, the word coping is very subjective.

BELIEVE IT OR NOT, there are between 400- 600 strategies. They are split into three areas, appraisal-focused with denial being the most common in this area. Then second is problem-focused, where you may modify your behaviour to cope and finally emotion-focused. This is where you alter your emotions to eliminate stress, e.g. relaxation. Just for a second; there think about you and what you may do?

This may affect your self-esteem. What is self-esteem? It basically means; your personal subjective evaluation of your own self-worth. Self-esteem covers emotional states, beliefs about oneself, despair, shame, and pride. Self Esteem is a vast area, and something I hear consistently in my coaching sessions.

The key areas as coping mechanisms that we all use include Defensive, Adaptive, Avoidance, Attack, Behavioural, Cognitive, Self-harm, and Conversion. I am sure when you reflect for a second, some of these areas will mean something to you. In coaching, this is where you need to consider the client and what coping strategies they may use. As I said, Coping is a label; there is so much more that can be covered by this word and will always need investigating in your sessions. I think, as a coach, you need to hold any judgment and bias when you hear words and labels.

Some of the strategies that people use to help themselves include are humour, seeking support, relaxation, and exercising. Now spend a few minutes reflecting on yourself and how many of these do you already do then think about the people around you and what you notice in them.

In summary, coping means investing in one's conscious effort to solve personal and interpersonal problems in order to try to master, minimise, or tolerate stress and conflict.

AWARENESS AND REFLECTION IS **KEY** TO NOTICE YOUR COPING STRATEGIES.

30

JOURNEY IN LIFE, A GREAT AREA TO REFLECT ON, WHO ARE YOU?

I recently found myself responding to my son in a conversation saying the words, "Be who you are and not what you think you should be." Be an individual and someone not conditioned to be a certain way; it is all about you being you. Have you ever reflected on your journey in life how often are you... YOU?

HAVE you ever thought and reflected on you and the changes? Have you ever thought about the differences and why? The conditioning that takes place through life, what has happened to you and are you entirely happy with your journey and who you are? An example of this, a small area but an interesting preference in me is how different I have been between the organisation, planning vs the last-minute casual, spontaneous me over time. Such a difference in me from when I was 18 compared to me now (not sharing my age). How conditioned I have become over the years with planning and organisation, but what is really me?

I CAN REMEMBER at 18 buying a monthly railcard to travel around Europe, the old western Europe at £126. A month travelling on any train around any of the countries in western Europe. The approach I had then compared to what I would do now or would have done ten years ago is widely different. At 18, I bought a rucksack and went, no planning, no accommodation no itinerary. I just went and went with what happened, very able to improvise, that was part of the fun.

The 18-year-old approach compared to me now is unbelievable. I reflect on the long-haul holidays I now do, the planning I now do down to restaurants I want to try, turning up at the airport three hours before the flight, almost too organised. Listening to my son who always gets anywhere with two minutes to spare made me laugh when he said I consider anything more than 5 minutes waiting a waste of my life. I could not argue with that.

I smiled so much with this response, this was me years ago and what a nice way to be, relaxed and having the ability to go with whatever presents itself. Over the years, how much conditioning has there been on me and then how I have probably tried to push my way on to my son (clearly not worked). I am so curious now he is older how I am going to change again. I am a lot more relaxed about things, and I wonder how much responsibilities in life change you and how much more draining this may be on you as a person. I have changed again. Thankfully, being relaxed is a lot less stressful.

This is just one tiny area I have reflected and the change in me. I reflect in a much more intense way and look at all the different directions I have chosen in life and why. I feel the thing to notice is you and why you have changed. Then with the changes how much of 'you' do people see, who is the real 'you'. I think the real 'you' is the most powerful and the most credible.

LIFE IS A GIFT AND WE ALL HAVE A RESPONSIBILITY TO MAKE THE MOST OF IT, SO THAT WHEN WE LOOK BACK, WE KNOW IT WASN'T WASTED.

Use the reflective log to reflect when something has gone wrong or there has been an issue in your life. Ask yourself these questions:

Q1 - WHAT IS HAPPENING AND WHAT DO YOU NOTICE?

Q2 - WHAT WERE YOU THINKING AND FEELING? HOW DID YOU BEHAVE DURING THE EXPERIENCE?

Q3 - WHAT ARE THE MAIN LEARNING POINTS FOR YOU FROM THE EXPERIENCE?

Q4 - HOW IS YOUR LEARNING GOING TO BE APPLIED IN THE FUTURE, WHAT MAY YOU DO DIFFERENTLY?

AFTERWORD

Thank you for reading Self Coaching for Personal Development. I know that if you apply areas we have discussed little changes will already be taking place and through repetition and change your mindset will grow.

MEET THE AUTHOR

CLAIRE MOODY

Claire is an extremely experienced trainer and coach at and you can always guarantee she will deliver outstanding results. She is incredibly passionate about both her training and coaching.

Having over 35 years' experience in training, coaching and quality assurance roles, Claire has experience as a teacher, trainer and coach with clients throughout the planet. She holds an MSc in executive coaching and is accredited by Ashridge, a world leader in executive coach training and development.

> *"It's not about being the best, it's about being the best you can be"*
> CLAIRE MOODY

HAVE QUESTIONS?

C/O Target Training Associates
107 Cheapside, London, EC2V 6DN
0800 302 9344
info@targettrg.co.uk
www.targettrg.co.uk
www.jcrm.shop

SOME OTHER TITLES IN THE JOURNAL SERIES

Coaching Journal
Law of Attraction Journal
Being Positive Journal
Improve Self-Esteem Journal
Do I or don't I deal with conflict Journal
Action Planning Journal
Management Journal
Rainbow Foods Journal

Contact us for a quote for a bespoke journal for your particular organisation

Personal coaching skills to reach your goals.

A coaching mindset is critical for creating a coaching culture and Coaching Mindset will assist you in many areas where coaching skills work best.

"A brilliant read. I am studying to become a personal trainer and I found that this book helped me better understand coaching, and what it means to be a coach." C Kelsey

"From personal growth to improving coaching technique, a great bitesize reflective tool." D Gabriele

Visit our website https://jcrm.shop/books/pre-order/ to read further and ordering information.

Your FREE Book Is Waiting

Many people struggle with low confidence and low self-esteem, which affects their professional and personal lives. Your thoughts and feelings have a significant impact and this is where issues can manifest. If we don't do something about it, a lack of confidence will hold you back. This book will give you an opportunity to think about your confidence in a different way.

Get your FREE copy:
www.jcrm.shop

www.ingramcontent.com/pod-product-compliance
Lightning Source LLC
Chambersburg PA
CBHW061816250726
48657CB00001B/452